Hop, Hop, Kanga...

Written by Saviour Pirotta
Illustrated by Caroline Church

Collins *Educational*
An imprint of HarperCollins *Publishers*

The little kangaroo's sister could hop over a rock.

His mum could hop right over a bush.

But the little kangaroo couldn't hop at all.

"Don't worry," said the little kangaroo's mother. "You will soon find your hop." "But I want to find it *right now*," said the little kangaroo. He looked for his hop under some stones.

He searched for it in the bushes.
But he could not find it anywhere.
"Grandpa will know where it is," thought
the little kangaroo. So off he went.

Before long the little kangaroo came to a tree trunk blocking the road. "Hop, hop, kangaroo," squawked the parrots in the trees.

"I haven't found my hop yet," said the little kangaroo.
And he climbed over the trunk.

A bit later the little kangaroo came to
a large patch of flowers.
"Hop, hop, kangaroo," buzzed the bees.

"I can't hop yet," said the little kangaroo.
And he tip-toed through the flowers.

Next the little kangaroo came to a river.
"Hop, hop, kangaroo," burbled the fish.
"I haven't found my hop yet," cried the
little kangaroo.

And he swam across the river.

The water was nice and cool.
The little kangaroo shook himself dry and
walked on until he came to a gate.
"Hop, hop, kangaroo," bleated the sheep.

Hop, hop,
kangaroo!

"I'd love to," panted the little kangaroo.
"But I haven't found my hop yet."
And he squeezed through the gate.

Soon the little kangaroo came to a large haystack.
"Hop, hop, kangaroo," mewed the farm cats.
"But I haven't found my hop yet," the little
kangaroo said miserably as he burrowed
through the hay.

"That was hot work," thought the little kangaroo.
He pulled the hay out of his fur and hurried along.

At last he came to a cornfield.
"Hop, hop, kangaroo," called the farmer.
"I haven't found my hop yet," cried the little kangaroo.

And he crawled through the corn
until he came to Grandpa's field.

"Hello," said the little kangaroo. "Do you know where my hop is?"

"I'm afraid I don't," Grandpa replied.

"Oh dear," sobbed the little kangaroo.

"I've looked for it everywhere. Where could it be?"

The little kangaroo was so hot and tired
he didn't look where he was sitting.
"Look out!" everyone cried.
But it was too late.

The little kangaroo sat right on top of a prickly bush.

"Ouch!" he cried. And he...

hopped right up into the air.

"Hey," Grandpa said. "You've found your hop."
"Yes," said the little kangaroo happily. "It was sitting right on top of this bush all the time."

And he hopped all the way home to tell his mum.